EVERYDAY ROUTINE

POEMS FROM NEW YORK TO PARIS

AMIR ALI SAID

Superchamp Books SB

New York

Everyday Routine, Poems from New York to Paris
By Amir Ali Said

Copyright © 2017 by Amir Ali Said.

A Superchamp Books First Paperback Edition

All rights reserved.
No part of this book may be reproduced in any form by any electronic or mechanical means, including information storage and retrieval systems, without the expressed written permission of the publisher, except by a reviewer, who may quote brief passages in a review. Published by Superchamp Books, Inc. P.O. Box 20274, Brooklyn, New York 11202-0274. www.superchampbooks.com; Twitter: @SuperchampBooks; @amiralisaid; Facebook: Superchamp Books

Editor: Amir Said

Photographs:
Cover photo by Isaiah Izzy George © 2017 Isaiah Izzy George
Back Cover photo of author by Amir Said © 2017 Amir Said

Cover, Design, and Layout by Amir Said

Print History:
December 2017: First printing.

Everyday Routine, Poems from New York to Paris / by Amir Ali Said
1. Said, Amir Ali 2. Poetry 3. New York City—Culture 4. Paris—Culture 5. New York City—Social Aspects 6. Paris—Social Aspects 7. Popular Culture—United States 8. Popular Culture—France I. Title

Library of Congress Control Number: 2017918939
ISBN 978-0-9997306-38

For my father, Amir Said.
Pop, thank you for my training and for reminding me
to never lose sight of QSYT.
Insha'Allah…Al-Humdullilah.

CONTENTS

INTRODUCTION	1
PART 1: SOCIAL COMMENTARY	7
Muscle Memory	8
Pale Whisper	9
How they Gonna Fix the Whole Shit?	10
Loneliness is Bliss	11
Fashion Weak	12
What Life Could Have Been	13
To Grow Old	14
The Two Seas	15
Manage the Heat	16
Tu Parles Anglais?	17
PART 2: NARRATIVE POEMS	18
Le Chat	19
Dale Went to Yale, Mitch Went to Penn	20
Help Me	21
5AM Outside Le PomPon	22
Shady Navy	23
Riley, Come Play with Me	24
Suffer	25
As Seen on the A Train Past Midnight	26
MK2 Bibliothèque	27

My Uber was Going Way Too Fast	28
The Beauty of a Day	29
Have You Ever Seen?	30
Getting on the Metro	31
The Globe Light	32
The Coffin Salesman	33

PART 3: LISTEN CLOSELY	**34**
Stop & Clutch	35
Mister Brown Tiles	36
Dying Oak Trees	37
Mr. Prime Time TV Show, Stop What You're Doing	38
Marching	39
Bullshit	40
Justice	41
I Spent My Last Dollar	42
Hey Black Girl (A Poem for Pe'Tehn)	43
If Only Somebody Would've Told Me	44
Bottle Cap	45
Right In Front of Me	46
You, In the NFL, Play Past These Things	47

PART 4: LOVE EXPERIENCES	**48**
Your Heart Cold	49
Reciprocals	50
She Wept, then She Cried	51
Those Same Piano Strings	52

And Someday It'll Just Be One	53
I Saw My Ex at Broadway-Lafayette	54
We Did What we Had to Do	55
No Such Thing	56
Posted Up	57
PART 5: PERSONAL MEMOIRS	**58**
I Remember Latin Souls	59
Steak, Mac and Cheese	60
Back in Brooklyn	61
Talking with Joel Barish	62
Gauchos Gym	63
Driving a Car on the Set of Be Kind Rewind	64
Galaga and Ms. Pacman	65
The Symphony	66
In Rucker Park	67
A Poem for Joe Walsh	68
I Listened to Grime One Day	69
Theater Kids Waiting Inside the Casting Office	70
I Took the L Train Everyday	71
Yo, What Happened to Peace?	72
ACKNOWLEDGEMENTS	**75**

Introduction

I was fifteen years old when I wrote my first poem, "Spark Plug." It was born out of an impromptu writing exercise my father gave me. He briefly left the room, giving me space to tackle the exercise (as he often did). When he came back in the room, he read my poem aloud, and I could hear the joy in his voice from reading it. Seeing the pleasant surprise on his face, I could feel how happy he was. Right then, I knew that I needed to continue writing and studying poetry.

At sixteen, I wrote and published my first book, *Performance Day*. It was a collection of short stories, poems, film criticisms, and other writings. This milestone encouraged me to deepen my understanding of poetry. I started studying the works of Sam Greenlee and Gil-Scott Heron. Greenlee's *Ammunition: Poetry and other Raps* played a pivotal role in my development as a writer; and listening to Scott-Heron's "The Revolution Will Not Be Televised" — and the rest of the *Pieces of a Man* album — also had a huge impact on me. Also, the writing exercises that my father was giving me were increasingly tailored to develop my poetry skills.

At seventeen, I was finished with homeschool. (Several years earlier, in my second semester in 8th grade, I left the New York City public school system for more independence.) At that time, the colleges I was most interested in going to were NYU and The New School. But after my father took me on a surprise trip to Paris, things changed. While we were in Paris, we talked a lot about our future (a regular thing for us). He reminded me that I had been writing about the French director Francois Truffaut when I was twelve years old. We had seen Truffaut's *The 400 Blows* together at BAM Cinema when I was younger, and it was that film that drew me further into French cinema.

In Paris, my father had gone to London for work one day and left me alone because he said he wanted me to see Paris by myself. While spending time alone in Paris, I discovered a city that was more broadly welcoming than New York. And even though I'm a New Yorker — which is to say, I can roll with all the toughness that the city has — New York, especially for black people, felt too segregated and stifling. So, six months after visiting Paris, I was back there and enrolled at EICAR International Film School.

When I moved to Paris, poetry became my therapy. Since I lived alone, my poetry was who I often spoke to at night and who I woke up to in the morning. I was adjusting to a new country, a new culture, and a new way of living. At times I was struggling. I was shedding my teen years and transitioning into my early twenties where a lot was thrown at me all at once. I was further from New York than I'd been my entire life, and poetry was one of the things that helped ease my transition.

Things further changed when I made my first visits back to New York. For the last three years, I've gone to New York one to three months out of the year, usually in the summer. These isolated visits have given me a new perspective and understanding of myself. I re-connected with my friends from Brooklyn and, in many ways, I rediscovered parts of myself when I was back in New York. This was big for me because, after my move to Paris, I had begun to distance myself from New York. There was left over anger in me from feeling stagnated. New York seemed more secluded and non-inclusive, whereas Paris seemed to have a more inclusive appreciation for all artists and writers; moreover the concept of race was much less in your face. Still, living in Paris for long periods and returning to New York showed me that I still loved New York. Although some of the negative aspects of New York (and America to a larger degree) were also amplified during these trips back home, they did help to reinforce who I am.

Everyday Routine is largely about my growth and experiences over the last four years — my time in Paris and my trips back home to New York in between. This book is guided by the philosophical, emotional, and physical changes I've encountered during this period. And the poems in this collection are also shaped by my evolving ideologies on life in general, social inequality, and politics.

About the Slant of the Poems in this Volume.

I have organized the poems in this volume into five parts: **Social Commentary, Narrative Poems, Listen Closely, Love Experiences**, and **Personal Memoirs**. **Social Commentary** contains some of the observations I've made about life in general. In this part, at times I dive into areas of humanity specific to the places I've lived (New York and Paris), and I highlight some of the personal thoughts and experiences that have shaped the way I view the world. **Narrative Poems** is a collection of poems that tell stories, that is to say, the poems in this part all work from the narrative form of poetry. **Listen Closely** is largely inspired by discussions I've had with my father about creating art that really grabs you. In this section, I dive into some of my thoughts on social activism, racism, inequality, and the joys and woes of humanity. **Love Experiences** chronicles my romantic relationships with women over the past six years. Finally, **Personal Memoirs** contains stories from my childhood, teenage years, and the present. This section also includes a number of poems dedicated to some of my favorite music. My music poems are generally inspired by the hip hop music that has influenced me over the years, and various poems in this part are inspired by actual hip hop songs.

    Amir Ali Said,
    Paris, France
    1 November, 2017

Social Commentary

Muscle Memory

My hands move different now.
The practice made a machine out of me;
I step up and analyze every beat.
I hear whistles the eye can't see.
The hardwood floors make me stronger
and the slickened pavement toughens my skin.
My feet are quicker.
I can almost run with the wind.
The sand and dirt that seep inside
create a welt of pain and pride.
When I get my sign, I slide.
My mind digs deeper.
I cycle through layers of information,
picking apart whichever page I'm in.

Pale Whisper

She comes in the darkness;
sharp, thin, and round.
She sticks when it's cold
and disappears when it's warm.
She glides and flies
but falls down in emptiness.
She tells tales of chilling yesterdays,
with swift movements through the night.
She fights the atmosphere;
and dissolves at the sight of heat.
She's a streak of a foreshadow.
A reminder of what's yet to come.

How they Gonna Fix the Whole Shit?

They can't fix the C train on Saturday at 4AM,
how they gonna fix the whole shit?
The 3 train has been down for repairs every weekend,
so how they gonna fix the whole shit?
I have never been on a B train without delays,
so how they gonna fix the whole shit?
I've never seen a repair notice for the E train,
so how they gonna fix the whole shit?

The L train only runs smooth during half its trip,
usually around the time the hipsters catch it,
so how they gonna fix the whole shit?
Transfer to the Z or the 7,
waiting all day long for the D ain't helpin'.
How they gonna fix the whole shit?
Cops ticket you for changing carts now.
Gentrifiers look at you, disdain on their brows.
How they gonna fix the whole shit?

Loneliness is Bliss

There is a certain freedom
in being alone.
A joy at times
in small victories.
Music is more enjoyable.
Life becomes a stagnant medium.
And you're alone,
you sit in your chair,
the only one there.

Fashion Weak

Women pile on street corners,
sidewalks, and alleyways.
Politicking, plotting, and scheming.
A rapper opens a door
and women flock like boars.
A bouncer filters out the elite groupies.

What Life Could Have Been

You put on a new face every day.
Your twins no longer look the same.
There's a southern disparity
and visible mental unclarity.

You've been broken for far too long.
Men have sung the same old songs.
You conform because your norm
has been neglected.
Seeking acceptance
from those you've been in bed with.
How would your three-year old self feel?
Running in Spiderman and Cinderella shoes.
Did you care back then?

Your inebriated affairs
cause you to lose sight of reality.
Who you once were
is a fraction of the casualties.
Your worth is tied to cosmetics
and social media diabetics.
You've missed out on what life could've been.

To Grow Old

To grow old is to feel thickened blood.
To smell connected memories sanded flood.
To hear the sounds of parties echo in the mud.

To grow old is to fight with measured pace.
To run with sharpened grace.
To jump from mountains of silent disgrace.

To grow old is to dive onto ships of chance.
To slip from the deck of withering fans.
To sit on hands of distant romance.

The Two Seas

Two seas exist in Paris.
A green Fujifilm adapter is attached
in the western quadrant.
A white and yellow light gleams
from the Octopus lamp,
next to the green candle
that's been asleep for hours.
Power chords lay ruined,
never to be used, never to be plugged in,
accompanied by a TV that never turns on
and a remote that remains idle.
Keys, pocket change, and Chapstick
lie down for the long nap.

Manage the Heat

Manage all the onslaughts,
fabrications,
expectations,
and accusations.
Decrease the heat,
steadily.
Apply a cold pack where directed,
decrease it some more.

Let the flame do its job.
If you ignite it,
it's bound to run wild;
it's meant to burn for some time.
Manage the heat,
manage the wave.
Before you know it,
the blaze is gone.

Tu Parles Anglais?

The tenor of my voice looms in the city,
my American tone tucked and sprayed
the gaze of men and women when they hear me say,
"tu parles anglais?"

Narrative Poems

Le Chat

She purred in the distance.
Isabelle danced as he watched.
"Once more," he said when she stopped.
She twirled and floated
while Le chat groaned and focused.
Her tutu was thin,
white lace, with blue ribbons.
Her ballet shoes weren't worn in yet,
but her big toe poked through.
She'd been distracted on her last turn
by the advance of another.
Le chat jumped in,
as she bled over the covers.

Dale went to Yale, Mitch went to Penn

It must be great having two
ivy league kids.
I mean, if Dale went to Yale,
and Mitch went to Penn,
you did great.
Even if Mitch didn't make it
the right way,
you still get credit
for doing well.
One for two is still fifty percent.
Mitch used a headset
and a number two pencil,
Dale used his black card to get in.
Even if Dale kills somebody
and Mitch steals cars,
they still got into Yale and Penn.

Help Me

My hair is disappearing
and my knees are flailing.
The new balance shoes aren't working,
neither is my Padres hat.
You remember when I bought these shorts?
They used to fit my waist.
Now the little boats are swimming on my legs.
My red shirt is no longer a small,
it fits like an extra large.
I can't hear anything
or feel my stress.
I can't taste my burger
or smell my death.

5AM Outside Le PomPon

It's 5AM outside Le PomPon,
the body guard says, "Bonne nuit."
It's chilly,
my body's warm,
and music pushes through the heat.
Charaf hops in his benz,
women spill into the streets.
As the drunks hail taxi's
for the after parties,
I zip up my jacket
and walk to the metro.

Shady Navy

It's dark and musty,
the pavement is crusted,
the road shallow.
The willow in the trees croaked
and the leaves crackled.
As the wind whipped,
the moon floated.
The worst of the night
remain shielded in shade.

Trench coats and boots,
pockets of jingling change,
distant memories fading each day.
Lint lay in disarray,
crumpled receipts lie tangled in despair.
An old pen sleeps without her top,
her estranged husband,
the silver doom of dinner accompanied her,
as the desk lay still.

Riley, Come Play with Me

There was an airswiper, a canister, and a belt.
The airswiper made sharp tic-tac-toe games
and the canister blew cold air with scented perfume.
The belt made welts.
"Riley! Come play with me," he yelled,
as his sister ran to the back.

"Pick one!" he said.
Her tic-tac-toe arm, on her third strike,
reached for the airswiper with all her might.
"Pick something else!" he urged.
With giggling ease, she picked up the canister
and released the cool breeze.
"Your go!" she screamed.

The belt had six loops,
a metal bar, and thick, rich brown leather.
When he snapped it,
the hide made the sound of a thousand levers.
He smirked as his arm turned red,
as Riley's wrist bled.
They laughed,
until he asked Riley,
"Do you want to play dead?"

Suffer

Her anemia
hurt her bulimic episodes.
She waltzed in dimmer pain
while her brother watched in shame.

Her parents weren't aware,
too far gone in the snow top mountain trails.
The split of proportions
opened old wounds
of babies made not born.

As Seen on the A Train Past Midnight

This train car smells like pickles and wood shavings.
And there is a bum sleeping, good,
underneath the map of the city.
In the corner, there is a lady with a toe-nail file.
She's sitting next to a man wearing
an "I Love NY" t-shirt, size extra small.
The bum awakes and begins yelling,
something about all of us
not having the right
to sit in his living room.
While the bum yells,
a man is break dancing to David Bowie.
I will change cars at Hoyt.

MK2 Bibliothèque

I smell the popcorn when I walk in.
The whiff of salt and butter,
with a hint of sugar sweetness.
I see the lady in her blue dress,
waiting for her date.
I hear a baby's laughter;
animated and in surround sound,
his laugh strikes me with memories.
I taste the Parisian air.
I feel the perspiration under my pullover.
I arrived late,
trying to keep it together,
because I hate missing the previews.

My Uber was Going way Too Fast

My Uber was going way too fast.
I just got off the L train and I needed a calm ride.
The concert earlier was cool,
but the fast-food wasn't all that.
I forgot what American processed was like.
In France, I got used to real nuggets and patties.

I had to roll the window down,
and no, I didn't let it all out.
I just needed a breeze,
some air to think,
Nascar's newest donor was driving.

Cab rides home are one of a kind.
You're commuting home with a stranger,
guiding you from the dangers
of midnight MTA travel.
There's a lot of trust
woven into these commutes.
That's why when you drive fast,
my awareness is acute.
Doesn't matter if Tony Stewart's your inspiration,
I'm gonna pay attention to that Uber map.
Because I'll roll out of this Camry at any second if I have to.

The Beauty of a Day

At times the sun wanders,
shedding rays of light across the sea.
The moon lays asleep,
as the stars awaken me.

Have You Ever Seen?

Have you ever seen
human paintings?
A truly beautiful woman?
A soldier with an MP5
on the train?
Have you ever seen
the bond between a dog
and a homeless man?
Have you ever seen
A woman smile at you
through darkness?
A drunk comedy show
on Rue De Rivoli?
Have you ever seen
a pregnant lady catch her baby?
Or a café goer sitting alone,
crying maybe?

Getting on the Metro

The green and white paint
chipped at the brim.
The grey handle in front of
the silver screen door
jolted open in front of me.
A twenty-something appeared.
As I stared into her eyes
and studied her face,
her body smiled at me.
She waved goodbye
as I said hello.

The Globe Light

While reading in bed,
I noticed the room get dimmer.
It felt like I was drifting into a hole
or an ancient well with rusted bricks.
Darkness was inescapable
and I couldn't scale the walls.

I thought it was my imagination
or perhaps the book was too deep.
Maybe I drifted too far into the pages
or maybe I just needed sleep.

I waited a few seconds
to see if the room would get brighter.
The dimness stayed, so I grew quiet.
I went back to reading,
then I heard a pop.
The globe light blew out,
then my reading had to stop.

The Coffin Salesman

Men, women, and children die.
Some to war,
old age,
homicide,
suicide,
and other vices.

Families torn,
bridges burned,
wounds are forever branded.

For the coffin salesman,
the mourning of another
heals his billing woes.
Death feeds his ailing soul.
With each passing
comes chips of cash.
Death spawns his beginnings.

Listen Closely

Stop & Clutch

On 34th Street
she clutched away
from the black man.
As her grey hair flailed in the wind,
she tugged and grunted,
looking at his suit with disdain.
He grinned.
"What's the problem?" she asked.
"You've always been."

Mister Brown Tiles

Mister brown tiles,
stapled into place,
aligned at the base.
Left astray,
stepped on for days.
I see you frown amongst the ground,
scarred and torn at the brow.

Dying Oak Trees

Snagged in a riverbank,
slain in a ditch.
Laid up on a reef,
hanging from ships.
Floating in water,
gasping in blind seas,
succumbing to the madness
of dying oak trees.
You are always peeking over your shoulder,
slicing your shadow into 8 million vestibules.

Mr. Prime Time TV Show, Stop What You're Doing

Stop making episodics labeled as us
that conveniently showcase you.
Stop emasculating
the one black guy on your show
and using sheep's wool to redefine us.
Stop appropriating shit you don't understand,
making it easy for the masses to get it mixed up.
Stop selling stepped on product.

Marching

Freedom is elusive.
Equality, temporary.
Injustice, pervasive.
Ethics are lacking,
virtues slacking,
and integrity's long taken a break.

Less feet and fists,
picket signs and protests.
Your mind marching,
testing the catch,
hoping to stir up a shift.

Bullshit

That is not your cousin
and you have not seen her in a movie.
She is not your future bae
and she'll never know you exist.
This party is not lit,
you just paid ten dollars to get in
and $30 for a bottle.
You did not get into Howard
to go to BMCC.
Music is not for you
and your friends know it too.
Last week you owed me fifty dollars
and this week you got new shoes.
Your girl is not Bad
and she barely fucks with you.

Justice

I think justice
looks like reparations
and a statement
that goes something like,
"We fucked up the parents
and grandparents,
the embryos too."

I Spent My Last Dollar

She had five cents in her bucket
as she looked at me
through her disintegrating winter coat.
Her dried tears were frozen
as she rocked herself to warmth.
The bed was a rusted shade of grey.
Her dog whimpered in the wind.
I didn't have anything to give them
because I spent my last dollar at the store.

Hey Black Girl (A Poem for Pe'Tehn)

Hey Black Girl,
keep doing your thing.
Build on this attention,
innovate upon your success.
Hey Black Girl,
study Sam Greenlee, Gil-Scott Heron,
and the vets.
Read about philosophy.
Continue writing and thinking.
Hey Black Girl,
be you.
Run under sprinklers,
play double-dutch,
and patti-cake.

If Only Somebody Would've Told Me

If only somebody would've told me
that I didn't have it all figured out.
That I had a long way to go.
That I should humble myself.
That I should never get too comfortable.
That practice makes better,
but never perfect.
That irrelevant people are best left alone.
Or that sometimes, some people
are just meant for memories.
If only Pop would've told me
once more again.

Bottle Cap

You sit and watch the particles
wiggle for space,
equating it to your own life
of withering waste.
People, the bubbles, are rising.
Running away from each other,
they float to the stop with speed;
ignoring their desires,
casting away their needs.
It is almost over,
your choice all but disappeared;
you allow the bottle cap to remain,
conquered by your fear.

Right In Front of Me

I woke up one day
and I couldn't see.
The world was still white
and the sun shined brighter.
I squinted to gain vision,
my lack of sight grew tighter.
Running to the bathroom,
half asleep, I struggled to see,
everything that was right
and there in front of me.

You, In the NFL, Play Past These Things

You, fortunate enough to be
the NFL, play past your stingers;
that hit wasn't that bad.
Play past your ankle sprain;
all you did was tweak it.
Play past that Achilles tenderness;
it's sore, but you can still run on it.
Play past that broken arm;
just throw a cast on.
Play past that neck pain;
you can fuse it back together later.
Play past the slip discs
and the broken ribs;
just rest and sleep on it,
you'll be fine by gameday.
Play past your shoulder separation;
pop it back in and let's go.
Play past that concussion,
you're fine, for now, anyway.

Love Experiences

Your Heart Cold

It's two in the morning.
Today, I'll admit,
was the first day
I thought to apologize.
We ended terribly.
Pride and lies.
If I spoke sooner.
I should've tried more.
Now it's too late.
These words frivolous.
Your heart cold.
mine, simmering.

Reciprocals

Attractions weakened,
we ain't speakin'
and I'm fine with that.
Your mother probably hates me,
your sister too.
At this point,
it's just reciprocals.

She Wept, then She Cried

She wept, then she cried.
the tears rolling out of her eyes.
The madness of it all
and the burning inside.
Two long months of disarray,
our anniversary one day away.
The pictures and feelings scaling the walls,
the hidden resentment and depression starting to fall.

Those Same Piano Strings

I listened to Jazz the other day.
The Piano strings tugged at my heart.
I remembered what you told me over dinner.
And I realized you lied.
My friends told me they saw you
with someone else.
You yelled, denied, and cried.

You told me you locked yourself in a bathroom;
that there was a knife and pills
inside there with you.
You had options.
I talked you down for hours,
trying to keep you with me.
Around four in the morning,
you opened the door.

Months later, we were still arguing.
About trust and other things.
Nothing actually happened, on my end,
Or yours (as far as I know).
But we were
young and unknowing.
It made sense why we split.
I thought of you today,
as I heard those same piano strings
playing in a Parisian café.

And Someday It'll Just Be One

I don't ever wanna watch
a marriage breakdown.
I don't ever wanna see
my mother or my father frown.
I struggle to understand
why things have to be some ways.
I get it, but some things
just will never be the same.
Like when, three becomes two,
and someday it'll just be one.
Or if three never became two,
and we'd stick with how things begun.

I Saw My Ex at Broadway-Lafayette

I saw my ex at Broadway-Lafayette.
I was running up the stairs
to beat the summer heat.
When she turned around,
we stared at each other
for a few beats.
"As if my day couldn't get any worse,"
she laughed.
"How are you?" I smiled.
Her awkward smile a reminder
of what had become.
There was some small talk,
of where she worked (nearby),
and me maybe stopping by.
Then as soon as we'd met
on Broadway-Lafayette,
I was back on my way,
never looking back,
wondering if she did the same.

We Did What we Had to Do

It was a year ago.
The first or maybe second argument.
It was the frequent disagreements.
The resentments and other leftover anger.

It was a stew of emotion
boiling for days.
It was six months ago.
A new change in our ways.
When the good was overshadowed;
The happiness drowning.
Outward darkness creeping into light.

It was the tears,
the fights,
and all the yelling at night.
It was three months ago.
It wasn't the distance.
It was just the stew;
by now, overcooked,
overflowing,
hot as ever.
And we did what we had to do.

No Such Thing

There is no such thing as mistakes,
wrong steps,
or wrong choices.
No such thing as regrets.
misspoken words,
or misunderstood vernacular.
No such thing as pain,
or hurtful actions.
No such thing as the one,
or the right place,
or the right time.
No such thing as perfection.
All you've got
is this life that is.
And that shit throws a lot at you.

Posted Up

In the secluded darkness
I wander amidst the cackles and yells.
The shrewd tales of escapades
and drunken fables give rhythm to the air.
Across the room I see a black woman,
illuminated at the bar.
She orders a drink
and winks at me from afar.

Personal Memoirs

I Remember Latin Souls

I remember when nobody wanted me.
When I couldn't catch and I couldn't hit.
I remember struggling to find a team
because even no amount of money
could equal a good fit.

I remember being accepted.
Then baseball practice,
panting in the summer heat,
struggling to breath,
learning discipline,
when all I wanted was to eat.

I remember ground-balls to First Base.
Line-drives to Third.
Home-runs to right field.
I remember getting thrown out at Second
and stealing home the next inning.
I remember the smell of the grass
and the dirt in the stains.
I remember sunflower seeds
and Jesse's old maroon Mercedes.

I remember Double-Time.
Little-Man.
Larry, and Jojo.
I remember my championship in slow-mo.
The rain of celebration.
But what I remember
most of all are those conversations
with Pop after games,
those days that my life changed.

Steak, Mac and Cheese

The scent of your masterpieces
linger with me.
My stomach growls
at the thought
of your cooking.
What do they know,
about your steak, mac & cheese?
My baseball meal?
My home-cooked birthday feast?
That clutch food
that every child needs.
Always perfected,
by my Ummee.

Back in Brooklyn

"Seen It All" in the speakers,
seen em fall, seen em leaking.
Ran down the stairs,
my audition was mad quick.
Authentic resume,
back in the crib for Madden.

Trooping through the boroughs
the Manhattan bridge.
Q train on my side
looking at the kid.
Windows rolled down,
man, I'm feeling the breeze.
Now I'm back in Brooklyn,
my mind's at ease.

Talking with Joel Barish

Backstage had a texture to it.
The wood smelled like salted cashews
and the wardrobe was fresh.
The pretty girls walked beside me
and coordinators ushered us through.
The atmosphere
of Hollywood-bound youth;
mothers gallantly prancing
in audience rows,
their children waving hello's.
That day everything changed.
The departure from CED to better things.
All thanks to Pop and Bonnie.
Soon, I was at Abrams,
then, talking with Joel Barish.

Gauchos Gym

I drank lemon-lime Gatorade for years,
before we switched to orange.
Even back in those days,
you said I showed no fear.
Cone drills to lay-up lines,
I can see it clear.
Practicing skills at two-sev,
when two kids rolled up and joined us.
We became neighborhood friends,
any day together they'd guard up.
Nobody knew it started in the living room,
pattering the rubber brown ball
on hardwood floors
in the wee hours of morning.
Puzzles scattered and tape still stuck today.
These were the Gaucho's days,
featuring my black head-band.
My short-lived journey to the NBA.

Driving a Car on the Set of Be Kind Rewind

Set breaks are fun.
You get some popsicles,
talk with crew,
and if you're fortunate,
an unlocked car will be there too.
Not a Ferrari or a Porsche, mind you,
but the set-built car.

You hop in the car built from scratch
and ask for one spin,
The engine will rev.
Nobody said you couldn't drive,
so why not?

In the driver's seat,
still in full wardrobe,
you'll feel cramped.
Enough room to reach the gas,
but you'll still sweat.
You start off slow,
then floor it.
The breeze will be elegant,
as you cruise down the street,
the crew laughing as you go by.
The car will move faster,
and you'll reach for the brake,
but you will crash
and hit the 2nd AD,
Because the break in this set-built car,
has not been installed yet.

Galaga and Ms. Pacman

Remember when we played
Galaga and Ms. Pacman?
Your favorite games.
This was before the PS2,
on that system I still can't remember.
I've got plenty of memories
of playing all the time.
From that bootleg racing game
to the baseball men that froze.
But, I always remember
Galaga & Ms. Pacman,
because we played and laughed for hours.
You'd always beat me in Ms. Pacman.
Sometimes you'd let me win,
but soon enough you were a kid again.
When Galaga came around,
I got my revenge.
Then we'd go eat some pizza.
And Pop would take us for a spin.

The Symphony

Inside the bar
the piano played.
Marley Marl shoutin' out
for Ace to rage.
Craig G rockin' out
with things to say.
Kool G Rap sparkin' up
the mic's ablaze.
Kane talkin' steady,
it's the only way.

In Rucker Park

I shot hoops at Rucker Park.
No, I didn't start
in any tournaments or showcases.
Mainly pick-up games
on the weekends
and horse, or twenty-one.
I had fun on this storied pavement,
unaware of the memories underneath.
But I put ball to gravel,
scored-lay ups and travelled
in Rucker Park.

A Poem for Joe Walsh

I've danced to your song
for seventeen years.
The one that comes after Luther gets it.
You know? When the Riffs found out
what really happened to Cyrus,
then Swan and the gang got a pass.
After Fox bit the rail
and Ajax got locked up.
Your song was perfect right there.
I needed to be uplifted
after all of that.
Cause I really didn't know
if the guys were going to make it
And there was four-year old me,
dancing in the mirror,
watching the credits roll,
singing the chorus of "In The City."

I Listened to Grime One Day

I listened to grime one day.
I started with Skepta,
then I listened to Stormzy.
Little Simz Krept on the mic
and Konan got a little noisey.
Tracksuit Mafia blared
through the speakers,
that's when things got Dizzee.
The whole Section stood up,
those dudes are real gritty.
Best in my city,
that's what Skengman said.
Chip caught a spiff of that,
now he wants Skengman's head.

Theater Kids Waiting Inside the Casting Office

I cringed at the sound
of the theater kids,
them full of fluff and flower,
their voices pretentious
and lively unreal.
When their names were called,
they sprang up
with wide smiles devoid of normality.
I imagine their auditions,
filled with up-speak
and precocious clutter.
Then, I'd watch them
walk out the audition room
failure in one hand,
an Adderall in the other.

I Took the L Train Everyday

I was three blocks
from New Lots.
The B15 was seven stops
from her twin.
The L train slept above,
running all night,
and churning in the morning.
Every class of people got on.
From winos to middle-schoolers
to Downtown executives
to Uptown drug rulers.
A cross section of culture.
Versions of fortune on display.
This is what I saw
when I took the L train everyday.

Yo, What Happened to Peace?

Puzzles on the ground
crossovers to the pounds.
Three's from tape.
The gaffer made me great.
Ummee walk in,
Pop let me stay up late.
Bumpin' Rakim
Eric B scratchin'
the Microphone Fiend
it make me feel relaxin.'

Acknowledgements

Pop (Amir Said), I could write an entire book about my gratitude and thanks to you, Alhumdulillah! Thank you for putting me in position to put the ball in play. Thank you for all of the advice, the discussions, and for teaching me how to be a thoughtful human being. I've learned so much from you since I entered this world. Thank you for being my hero. Finally, thank you for encouraging me to become a writer, an actor, and a filmmaker, and anything I've ever dared to imagine. Above all, I'm thankful to Allah for making you my father. Alhumdulillah!
Ummee (Qamar Said), Thank you most importantly for your love. Without you, Pop and I wouldn't have had Madden (and you know how important that was to us). Thank you for sending me pictures from my childhood to remind me who I am. Thank you for believing in me all these years. Thank you for Saturday night movies together as a family. Thank you for taking me to museums all over New York. Above all, I'm thankful to Allah for making you my mother. Alhumdulillah!
To my Brooklyn crew: Raheem "Rah," Thank you for your support, reliability, and for our timeless trips around New York City. Javon "Von," Thank you for always encouraging me and for rolling with me to events at the last minute. Asante "Te," Thank you for your support, advice, and friendship. Scott "Scotty," Thank you for being my wingman since we were fifteen. Nobody knew about me without knowing about you, we went everywhere. Jervon "Jerv," Thank you for always bringing up Inside Man when we're around girls so that it helps everybody in the crew. Caleb "Crob," Thank you for always adding insight and for being the calmest amongst us.
Thibaud, Thank you for your friendship, for taking me into your home, for always supporting me, and for helping me make it through EICAR. To Marianne Goarin and Jean-Michel Goarin (Thibaud's parents), Thank you for welcoming me into your home, I cannot tell you enough how much it meant to me. Mariella Gross, You are family. Thank you for helping make

EICAR possible. Thank you for taking me in. And thank you for giving me the chance to shoot my first concert in Vienna. Jake Lamar (EICAR), Your writing class was very helpful, thank you. Elizabeth Schub (EICAR), Thank you for providing your encouragement and a platform where I could further sharpen my creative ideas. Jamie Claar, Thank you for your support and understanding that every artist needs a bridge. Anna Zaborowska, Thank you for helping to hold down Superchamp Books. Charaf Tajer, There's no party like a Pigalle party! Thank you for having a club in Paris I could go to for the music I liked to hear and the kinds of people I needed to see.

About The Author

Amir Ali Said is a writer, actor, and filmmaker from Brooklyn, New York. His first book, *Performance Day*, was published in 2013, and in 2017, he co-edited *Best Damn Hip Hop Writing: The Book of Yoh* (Travis "Yoh" Phillips). Amir has been featured in several films and television shows, including *Inside Man*, *Game 6*, "The Dave Chapelle Show," and "Law and Order: Criminal Intent." He splits his time between New York and Paris.

www.ingramcontent.com/pod-product-compliance
Lightning Source LLC
Chambersburg PA
CBHW020622300426
44113CB00007B/744